# WHY THE RESURRECTION?

# WHY THE RES

# JRRECTION?

*A Personal Guide to Meeting the Resurrected Christ*

GREG LAURIE

*Tyndale House Publishers, Inc., Wheaton, Illinois*

Visit Tyndale's exciting Web site at www.tyndale.com





Cover designed by Dean H. Renninger

Interior designed by Harvest Design

Edited and researched by Harvest Publications



---

**Library of Congress Cataloging-in-Publication Data**

Laurie, Greg.
Why the Resurrection? a personal guide to meeting the resurrected Christ / by Greg Laurie. p. cm.
ISBN 1-4143-0321-1 (sc)
1. Jesus Christ–Resurrection. 2. Easter. 3. Jesus Christ–Appearances. I. Title.
BT482.L38 2004
232'.5–dc22 2004019549

---

Printed in the United States of America
08 07 06 05
4 3 2 1

# CONTENTS

*"And since we died with*

*Christ, we know we will*

*also share his new life. We are*

*sure of this because Christ*

*rose from the dead . . . ."*

Romans 6:8-9

# PREFACE: THE EVENT THAT CHANGED HISTORY

"THE STORY OF THE CHRIST DID
NOT END AT THE CROSS,
IT MERELY BEGAN THERE!"

Four hundred years before the birth of Christ, the renowned Greek philosopher, Socrates, drank the poison hemlock and lay down to die. One of his friends asked, "Shall we live again?"

The dying philosopher could only reply, "I hope so, but no man can know."

This is a question that every thinking person gets around to asking sooner or later. What will happen after I die?

The resurrection of Jesus Christ provides a resounding answer to the question of life after death. Because Jesus died and rose again bodily from the dead three days later, it means that we, as Christians, do not have to fear death. That is why Christ's resurrection from the dead is among the most important of biblical truths. The resurrection of Jesus, next to His crucifixion, is the most important event in all of human history. It sets the Christian faith apart from all others.

For more than two thousand years, the devil has been trying to discredit the resurrection of Jesus. The Resurrection spells his defeat. Satan knows that if you believe this great truth that Jesus rose bodily from the dead, then it will change your life.

In fact, more documents exist proving that Jesus has risen from the dead than documents proving that George Washington crossed the Delaware. We simply base our history upon the factual evidence we have, and the facts stack up. Jesus Christ rose from the dead.

It is interesting to note, though, that the nonbelievers of Jesus' day seemed to have more faith in His words than the believers did. Even though Jesus predicted He would rise again from the dead, it went right over the disciples' heads. They didn't get it at all. In contrast, the religious leaders who played a part in the death of Christ came to Pilate and said,

> Sir, we remember what that deceiver once said while he was still alive: "After three days I will be raised from the dead." So we request that you seal the tomb until the third day. This will prevent his disciples from coming and stealing his body and then telling everyone he came back to life! If that happens, we'll be worse off than we were at first." (Matthew 27:63-64)

Pilate assigned guards to the tomb and made it as secure as possible. Obviously, the enemies of Jesus remembered His words more clearly than His followers did. They had this fear that He would do what He said He would do. Of course, He did rise again from the dead. As the believers were worshipping the risen, living Christ, the nonbelievers were plotting to destroy the witness of the resurrection of our Lord.

The enemies of Jesus spread the rumor that His disciples stole the body. Some even to this very day will say they hold to that viewpoint. But if you carefully consider that theory, you will quickly realize it does not hold water. Consider this: Every one of the apostles of Jesus (with the exception of John) went to an early grave because they could not and would not deny what was true. The truth is that Jesus Christ had been raised from the dead.

The reason people today say they don't believe that Jesus rose from the dead or don't believe in the teachings of Jesus is because they know, deep down inside, that if they believed these things, they would have to change the way that they live. Jesus said, "Their judgment is based on this fact: The light from heaven came into the world, but they loved the darkness more than the light, for their actions were evil" (John 3:19).

The Apostle Paul tells us if Christ has not risen then our faith is in vain. But He did rise! The Christian faith is founded upon that promised event. Thank God He left that tomb and came into our hearts as we embraced Him as Savior and Lord. It was Augustine who said, "He departed from our sight that He might take residence in our heart. He departed, and behold, He is here."

To enhance your studies of God's Word, I have developed this book, *Why the Resurrection?* As a companion to *Why the Passion?*, it is my hope that this volume will help you remember and reflect on the great hope not only found in Christ's death, but also in His resurrection. You may want to use it for devotions as you read through the accounts of the Resurrection and the immediate events that took place thereafter. It's also the perfect resource for refreshing your memory on the main events and people of the Resurrection. I hope that it will be a book you will use for years to come, and also a resource you can share with your family and friends during Easter or whenever you are sharing the hope found in the resurrection of Jesus Christ. Because the story of Jesus Christ did not end at the cross, it merely began there!

Shall we live again? As followers of Jesus Christ, we can know, without a doubt, that we will. He has risen. He has risen indeed!

# HOW TO USE THIS PERSONAL GUIDE

I desire *Why the Resurrection?* to be an easy-to-use reference for your spiritual growth.

*Alphabetical Order of Topics*

In the chapters "People of the Resurrection" and "Places of the Resurrection," each topic is listed alphabetically for quick and simple referencing.

*Cross-references*

To help you easily find information in this personal guide, I have provided you with two forms of cross-references:

1. You will encounter asterisks (*) after the first entry of key topics found elsewhere in the chapter you are reading. These asterisks appear to let you know you can read another article on this topic in the same chapter. For example: "the apostles*" directs you to another section in "People of the Resurrection" entitled "The Apostles."
2. You will find cross-references within parentheses by topics that also are discussed in other chapters of this biblical guide. For example: "the Mount of Olives (see 'Places of the Resurrection')" lets you know that this topic is discussed within another chapter called "Places of the Resurrection." However, due to the frequency in which the name *Jesus Christ* appears, cross-referencing (in this manner) every occurrence of the Lord's name has been avoided.

*"Why are you looking in a tomb for someone who is alive? He isn't here! He has risen from the dead!"*

Luke 24:5-6

# WHAT HAPPENED EASTER MORNING

"VERY EARLY ON SUNDAY MORNING, EVERYTHING CHANGED. HOPE HAD ARISEN!"

The December 6, 1999 cover of *Time* featured a painting of Jesus Christ (see "People of the Resurrection") that introduced a series of articles about His impact not only on our time, but also on all of humanity for all time. Reynolds Price, the writer of one of the articles, made this statement: "A serious argument can be made that no one else's life has proved remotely as powerful and enduring as that of Jesus."

That is true. There has never been, nor will there ever be, anyone like Jesus. He stands out from all others. Because Christ died and rose again, His life proved to be powerful and enduring. His death and resurrection transformed the world and the lives of those who believed on Easter morning, and continually transforms the lives of those who believe today.

## LOST IN TRANSLATION

I am always amazed at how diverse the English language is. When I was in England some time ago, I noticed some windows with large posters that read, "BILL STICKERS WILL BE PROSECUTED." I thought, *Who is Bill Stickers, and what has he done?* When I asked someone about it, I discovered (a few laughs later) that "bill stickers" are people who put up posters illegally. Sometimes things get lost in the translation.

That is what happened to the followers of Christ after His crucifixion. Jesus had spoken to the disciples about His impending death and resurrection constantly and in great detail. Nevertheless, the disciples incorrectly thought Christ was going to overthrow the Roman government and establish an earthly kingdom. Therefore, the dreams of the disciples were destroyed when they saw Jesus crucified on a Roman cross. The One called the King of kings was taken and crowned with thorns. They saw spikes driven through His hands and feet. They hoped for a last-minute miracle. But none came. Their Lord was dead. The disciples never anticipated the Crucifixion. They misunderstood the message—it was lost in translation.

But very early Sunday morning, three days after Joseph of Arimathea laid Christ in the tomb, Jesus' message became clear. Let's read about what happened that first Easter Sunday in Luke 24:1-12:

> But very early on Sunday morning the women came to the tomb, taking the spices they had prepared. They found that the stone covering the entrance had been rolled aside. So they went in, but they couldn't find the body of the Lord Jesus. They were puzzled, trying to

> think what could have happened to it. Suddenly, two men appeared to them, clothed in dazzling robes. The women were terrified and bowed low before them. Then the men asked, "Why are you looking in a tomb for someone who is alive? He isn't here! He has risen from the dead! Don't you remember what he told you back in Galilee, that the Son of Man must be betrayed into the hands of sinful men and be crucified, and that he would rise again the third day?"
>
> Then they remembered that he had said this. So they rushed back to tell his eleven disciples—and everyone else—what had happened. The women who went to the tomb were Mary Magdalene, Joanna, Mary the mother of James, and several others. They told the apostles what had happened, but the story sounded like nonsense, so they didn't believe it. However, Peter ran to the tomb to look. Stooping, he peered in and saw the empty linen wrappings; then he went home again, wondering what had happened.

I love the way Luke begins this chapter: "But very early on Sunday morning" (verse 1). Here humanity had done its worst. Christ was put to death. The disciples left the cross dismayed and disillusioned, the religious leaders rested in victory, and the Christ lay dead and buried in a dark garden tomb. Everything had fallen apart. But very early on Sunday morning, everything changed. Hope had arisen.

Then the female disciples of Christ came to the tomb, taking the spices they had prepared. Notice that it was the women—not the men—who were last at the cross and first at the tomb. The men were in hiding, but the women were willing to stand up for the Lord. The men were sleeping, but the women were willing to care for the

Lord's body. Mark's Gospel tells us that Mary Magdalene, Salome, and Mary the mother of James (see "People of the Resurrection") were present among the women (see Mark 16:1). They were there to anoint His dead body. Though He was dead, their love for Him refused to dim. Their faith in Him had not failed. What they had hoped for simply had not happened. Yet those faithful followers would not abandon His dead body. They honored Him even in death.

The faithfulness of the women rewarded them with an unexpected surprise. Instead of finding the dead body of Jesus, they came face to face with holy angels of God. Then one of the angels said, "He isn't here! He has risen from the dead! Don't you remember what he told you back in Galilee, that the Son of Man must be betrayed into the hands of sinful men and be crucified, and that he would rise again the third day?" (Luke 24:6-8). Then they remembered His words. So they ran to tell the apostles (see "People of the Resurrection"). But when the apostles heard what had happened, they said that the story sounded like nonsense, so they would not believe it (see verses 10-11). These great men of faith regarded the witness of the women as mere hysteria. It's hard to believe that these were the apostles. These were the ones whom Jesus spent an entire night praying over before He called them. Yet when they heard the message that the Lord had risen, they didn't believe it.

## THE RACE TO THE TOMB

The Gospel of John fills in a few details that reveal that two disciples investigated Mary Magdalene's testimony. To their credit, Peter and

John (see "People of the Resurrection") had to see the empty tomb for themselves. After hearing about the resurrection, Peter and John sprinted to the tomb, but John outran Peter (see John 20:1-4). I think there is a reason why John beat Peter to the tomb, and it had little to do with who was the faster runner.

Consider this: Remember when you were a child and you got into trouble with your mom and she uttered those ominous words: "You just wait until your father gets home!" Then when dad pulled into the driveway, I bet you did not run as quickly to meet him at the door. You knew you were going to have to come face to face with what you had done wrong. Your conscience was guilty and you feared the consequences of your actions.

In the same way, Peter's last contact with the Lord was when he denied Him. He was running to the tomb, but with mixed emotions to say the least. Then Peter walked into the tomb. With his chest heaving from the run, he probably thought, *What's going on here? Where is the Lord? Where is His body?* Then John entered, and the Gospel tells us that "he saw and believed—for until then they hadn't realized that the Scriptures said he would rise from the dead. Then they went home" (John 20:8-10).

## DON'T LIVE IN THE OLD WAY

Now Peter and John were gone. The other women had left too. And there was Mary—all alone. She was still wondering where the body of Jesus was. She could not take it anymore. She broke under the pressure and began to weep. So the angels in the tomb asked her, "Why are you crying?" (John 20:13). And she replied, "Because they have taken away my Lord . . . and I don't know where they have put him" (John 20:13).

Then hope came to Mary. She heard a voice speak to her out of the darkness. It was Jesus, but she did not recognize Him at first. " 'Why are you crying?' Jesus asked her. 'Who are you looking for?' " (John 20:15). She answered and said, "Sir, . . . if you have taken him away, tell me where you have put him, and I will go and get him" (verse 15). Then Jesus said her name, "Mary." And she realized that He was the Lord and cried out, "Teacher!" (verse 16). She grabbed a hold of Him, but Christ told her, "Don't cling to me . . . for I haven't yet ascended to the Father. But go find my brothers and tell them that I am ascending to my Father and your Father, my God and your God" (verse 17).

Some people have tried to read some mystical meaning into this verse. They have claimed that the Lord's resurrected body was fragile and you did not want to touch it. That is not true. In other instances people touched Him. In Matthew's Gospel, after the Resurrection, the women grabbed a hold of Jesus' feet and worshipped Him. When He appeared to the disciples in the upper room and Thomas (see "People of the Resurrection") was there, Jesus told him to touch His hands and His side (see John 20:27).

I think there is a deeper meaning to why Jesus told Mary not to touch Him. It is better translated, "Don't cling to Me." Or literally, "Stop clinging to Me." Jesus was essentially saying, "Mary, it is a new day. It is not going to be the way it used to be. In the old days, I would be with you physically in a given place at a given time. We would spend time together. Those days are gone. Now it is going to be better. My Holy Spirit is going to live inside of you!" Then He tells her, "I am ascending to my Father and your Father, my God and your God" (John 20:17). Jesus was saying, "Mary, because of what I have done at the Cross and at the Resurrection, you can approach God as your Father." That was a revolutionary thought to the average Jew of the day. The Jews would refer to God by using the more formal term, *Lord.* They would rarely, if ever, use the intimate term of *Father.* Jesus was saying, "This is a new covenant that is established. Now I am going to send you My Holy Spirit. Don't cling to the old ways. Don't live in the old way. This is a new covenant I have established." This is true for all of us as well, for the Apostle Paul wrote, "For you did not receive a spirit that makes you a slave again to fear, but you received the Spirit of sonship. And by him we cry, '*Abba*, Father' " (Romans 8:15 NIV, emphasis mine).

The Bible says that Christ has done all of that for us. He has opened for us a new and a living way. Mary was so excited about seeing the Lord and hearing His message that she could not wait to tell the others. John 20:18 says, "Mary Magdalene found the disciples and told them, 'I have seen the Lord!' Then she gave them his message."

The message of Christ's resurrection transformed everything. It transformed a group of disillusioned, discouraged, and frightened women and men into bold and courageous disciples who turned their world upside down.

## LESSONS FROM EASTER MORNING

There are a number of things we should learn from that first Easter morning some two thousand years ago.

First, Easter reminds us that God loves ordinary and flawed people. They don't come any more flawed than Peter, John, and Mary. Remember, Mary was a demon-possessed woman—but Jesus healed her and transformed her life (see Luke 8:2). He not only forgave her but also commissioned her to go and take this message to the world. This gives hope to all of the ordinary people out there. You, who were picked last for the team. You, who never won the contest. You, who never distinguished yourself in any significant way from the others. This message from the Resurrection reminds us that God can do extraordinary things through ordinary people.

Secondly, Easter stands as living proof that God blesses those who seek Him with their whole heart. There is no question that Mary's persistent faith and love was richly rewarded. She was last at the cross. She was first at the tomb. She just wanted to be close to Jesus. She loved the Lord and wanted the world to know. She made time early in the morning to be with Him. If you will make time in your life and in your schedule for Jesus, He will reward you as well. The Bible says, "Great is his faithfulness; his mercies begin afresh each day" (Lamentations 3:23-24). But some of us will say, "I don't have time for Bible study or prayer. I have so many things to do." If that's the case, then maybe you need to slow down and make time for what is important. God will bless you for that. Mary made time for Jesus. What a blessing she received!

The third lesson we need to learn is that Easter reveals the promise that God will more than meet us halfway. Here was a woman who was weakened in her faith but strong in her love. She came with what she had and Jesus more than met her half way. Maybe you have a weakened faith? A tragedy has befallen you. A loved one has died. A marriage has collapsed. Your faith has suffered. Maybe in your estimation, you feel as though God has somehow let you down. God wants to renew your faith. He wants to bring you back to that place of fervency and commitment. Just as He ministered to Mary, He can minister to you as well.

Finally, Easter gives us hope for now and eternity. Mary was so excited because what appeared to have been the worst defeat imaginable, remarkably turned out to be the greatest victory of all. The fact that Jesus Christ rose from the dead means that there is hope in this life and hope after it.

In the words of the Apostle Paul, Easter supplies us with hope in this life because, "The Spirit of God, who raised Jesus from the dead, lives in you. And just as he raised Christ from the dead, *he will give life to your mortal body* by this same Spirit *living* within you" (Romans 8:11, emphasis mine). Paul is saying that God has provided every Christian with the power to live this life He has called us to live. I admit, living the Christian life can be hard, but it is possible through the power of the Holy Spirit. The same Spirit who raised Jesus from the dead has taken residence in you. The same Spirit whom Jesus breathed on the disciples is living inside of you. He will enable you to be the woman or man that God has called you to be.

But Easter also reveals the hope of life after death, because if Jesus died and rose again, we too will be raised like Him. The Apostle Paul made this point in his letter to the church in Corinth:

> But now Christ is risen from the dead, and has become the firstfruits of those who have fallen asleep. For since by man came death, by Man also came the resurrection of the dead. For as in Adam all die, even so in Christ all shall be made alive. (1 Corinthians 15:20-22 NKJV)

The Bible says that you are going to fall asleep and go into the presence of God. That is the picture Scripture uses. Because Jesus died and rose again, you have life beyond the grave. The Apostle Paul tells us, "For if we believe that Jesus died and rose again, even so God will bring with Him those who sleep in Jesus" (1 Thessalonians 4:14 NKJV). Whatever stage of life that you are in, this promise is precious. We, as believers, will live forever with God in heaven.

This is what happened Easter morning. God through Christ conquered sin and death, providing eternal life to anyone who believes. No other person's life–past, present, or future–has accomplished such a feat. There will never be anyone like Jesus, and because of what happened Easter morning we will have the privilege of spending eternity with Him.

*"You believe because*

*you have seen me.*

*Blessed are those who*

*haven't seen me and*

*believe anyway."*

John 20:29

# EVIDENCE FOR THE RESURRECTION OF CHRIST

"For all practical purposes, God says, 'Believe and I will show you.' "

Christ's resurrection from the dead is not a peripheral issue. The Resurrection is foundational to the Christian faith. In fact, it's what sets Christianity apart from all other faiths. For that reason, it's easy to see why people have attempted to explain away the Resurrection. But to the dismay of skeptics throughout history, four main lines of evidence exist that help attest to the truth of the Resurrection.

## THE EMPTY TOMB

The first argument for the Resurrection is the empty tomb. That Christ's tomb was empty three days after He died is essential to Christianity—for if Christ's body was still there, then Christ did not rise from the dead. And if Christ is not alive, then our faith is worthless (see 1 Corinthians 15:14). But one look at the Gospels and it is clear that all four authors were in complete agreement that Christ's tomb was empty three days after He died. Many other witnesses verified this fact as well (see Matthew 28:5-6; Mark 16:6; Luke 24:1-3; John 20:1-2).

The oldest claim against the Resurrection was that somebody stole the body of Christ. In fact, when someone supposes that Christ's body was stolen, they actually help prove the resurrection of the Lord. After all, only two groups of people had real motives to steal the body: the followers of Christ and the enemies of Christ. And from examining history and Scripture, neither of these groups were likely candidates for robbing the tomb of Christ.

Despite the arguments throughout history, the disciples were not likely suspects for counterfeiting the Resurrection. The truth of the matter is that the followers of Christ did not even believe Christ was going to rise from the dead. Remember when the women reported the Resurrection to the disciples? The Scriptures tells us that the men thought the report of the women "sounded like nonsense, so they didn't believe it" (Luke 24:11). Instead of waiting with great anticipation, they rejected it out of hand. It's also unlikely that the disciples—who just three days ago fled for their lives during the Crucifixion—would have suddenly mustered the courage and ingenuity to steal the body and then boldly begin preaching and teaching about a Jesus who was really dead. The facts simply do not match up. The disciples were in hiding. They were in shock and disbelief. None of Christ's followers exhibited the character it took to challenge the Roman government and steal the body of Christ. That is a dramatic change that cannot be overlooked.

The only other main suspects for the robbery of Christ's body were His enemies. The only problem with this theory is that Christ's enemies had no motive to rob His grave. The leading priests and other religious leaders put Christ to death because His teachings and His followers posed a threat to their religious system and way of life. The last thing these people wanted was another Jesus movement. That's why they had Christ crucified. And that's why the religious leaders went to great lengths to eliminate any appearance of a resurrection. The Gospel of Matthew tells us that they went to Pontius Pilate and said:

> Sir, we remember what that deceiver once said while he was still alive: "After three days I will be raised from the dead." So we request that you seal the tomb until the third day. This will prevent his disciples from coming and stealing his body and then telling everyone he came back to life! If that happens, we'll be worse off than we were at first. (Matthew 27:63-64)

Then Pilate replied, "Take guards and secure it the best you can" (Matthew 27:65). So they went and sealed the tomb and placed guards there to protect it (see Matthew 27:66). It sounds as though these religious leaders possessed more confidence in the resurrection of Christ than His own followers had.

The truth of the matter is that the religious leaders took extreme measures to protect Christ's body from being stolen. They wanted to prove that Christ's promise of a resurrection was a lie. The religious leaders left no room for error. They covered their bases to eliminate any chance of any stories circulating about Christ rising from the dead. Stealing the body would have accomplished everything the

The Garden Tomb in Jerusalem, the possible burial site of Jesus Christ

enemies of Christ were against. But if they had stolen the body, they undoubtedly would have produced it once that fledgling group of believers began to win people to Christ. But Jesus' enemies never produced His body, because they had no body to produce. The tomb was empty because Christ rose from the dead.

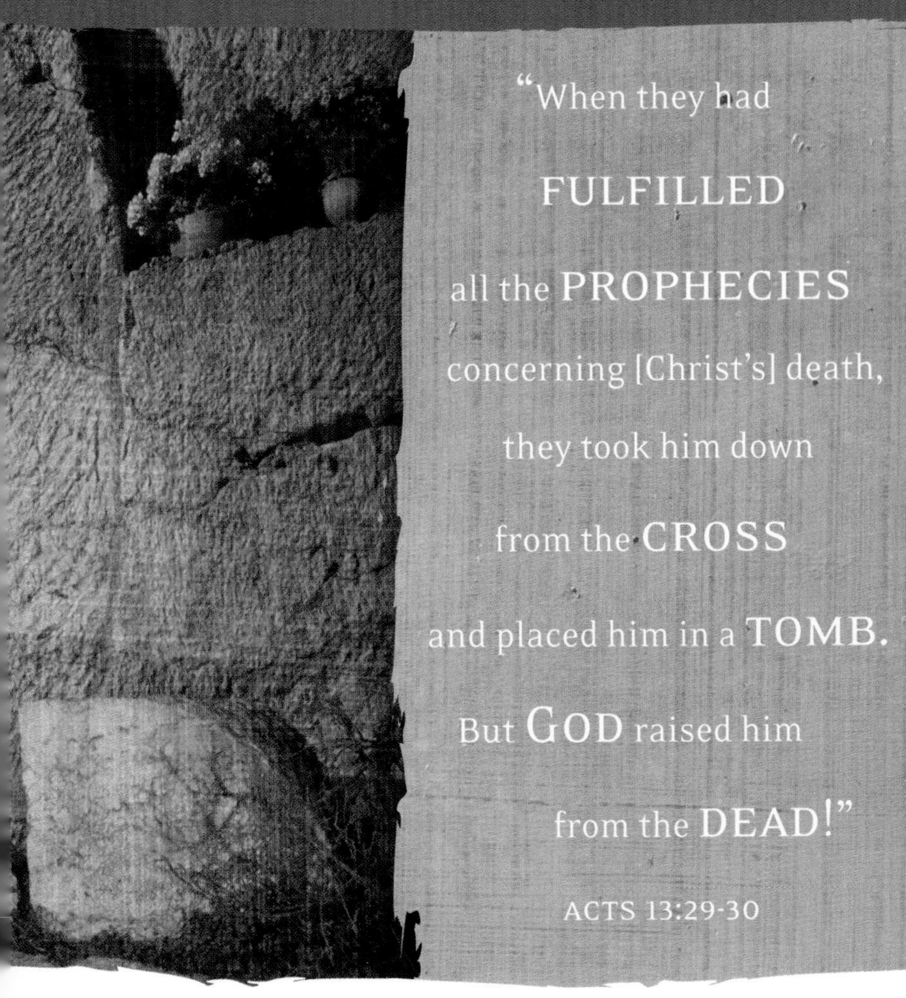
"When they had
FULFILLED
all the PROPHECIES
concerning [Christ's] death,
they took him down
from the CROSS
and placed him in a TOMB.
But GOD raised him
from the DEAD!"
ACTS 13:29-30

## THE APPEARANCES OF THE RISEN LORD

The eyewitness accounts of the risen Lord also attest to the truth of the Resurrection. The reality is that when Jesus was crucified, His disciples were devastated and destroyed. Their faith was to a large degree shattered. They had no hope of ever seeing Christ alive again. Yet Jesus not only appeared to the disciples on a number of occasions, He also appeared to five hundred people at one time (see 1 Corinthians 15:6).

Despite the historical documentation of these eyewitness accounts, people often claim that they are mere fabrication. But when you inspect the accounts of Christ's appearances, they look nothing like fabricated stories. Christ first appeared to Mary Magdalene. The same woman from whom Christ cast out seven demons (see Luke 8:2). To say the least, Mary was not your ideal character witness, and if you are making up a story, she would not be the first person you would have chosen.

Another notable detail is that all four Gospel writers agree that the women were the first people to receive the angelic announcement of the Resurrection. If you were fabricating a story about Christ, you probably would not have included the angel's announcement to the women. Why? Because the traditional Jewish understanding of Jesus' time was that the testimony of women was not accepted in legal situations (see Josephus, *Antiquities* 4.8.15 [219]). So if the disciples wanted to create a story that would deceive society, choosing one based on the testimony of women was less than ideal. A fictitious story only would have included men, for very few people during this time took into account the testimony of women. This strongly supports the validity of the testimonies concerning the appearances of Jesus Christ. The testimonies of the women, the disciples, and the five hundred eyewitnesses of the risen Christ are all true. Jesus the Christ had truly risen.

## THE MARTYRDOM OF THE APOSTLES

If the resurrection of Christ was a mere fairy tale, why would every one of the apostles go to an early grave for a lie? Experience tells us that whenever there is a conspiracy, someone always breaks. This is especially the case when the indictments start flying and the person knows they are going to serve some time. Someone will break. They always do. And when the first person does break, others will follow because everyone is out to try and save their own hide.

Similarly, if the apostles had stolen the body, why wouldn't they have broken the code of silence and simply confessed the truth? "We stole the body," they could have said, "And I'll tell you where it is!" But this didn't happen. In fact, the apostles not only held to their story, they even died for it. As we look over church history and tradition, every single apostle (with the exception of John) died gruesome and painful deaths, because they confessed the truth of the resurrected Christ:

- **Peter**: In Rome, Peter was severely scourged and then crucified upside down. He requested to be crucified upside down because he did not feel worthy to die in the same manner as his Lord.
- **Andrew** (brother of Peter): Andrew was martyred in Patrae, Achaia. It was there that he was bound to an x-shaped cross and crucified. He preached to his persecutors until he died.
- **James** (son of Zebedee): The first of the apostles to be martyred, James' death is the only martyrdom of the apostles mentioned in the New Testament (see Acts 12:2).

Herod Agrippa I, the grandson of Herod the Great, was responsible for beheading James.

- **John** (brother of James): Tradition tells us John was put in a caldron of boiling oil, but the oil mysteriously didn't harm him. Afterward, he was banished to the island of Patmos. Though John was sentenced to death because of his faith, he was the only apostle who did not die for his belief in the risen Christ.
- **Philip**: This apostle was martyred in Heliopolis. He was scourged and later crucified.
- **Bartholomew** (Nathanael): According to the "Martyrdom of St. Bartholomew," he was put in a sack and thrown into the sea. Another source claims he was crucified upside down after being flayed alive.
- **Thomas**: This apostle of Christ was killed in India with a lance that was run through his body.
- **Matthew** (the Tax Collector): Matthew was slain in Ethiopia.
- **James** (son of Alphaeus): The Apostle James was stoned and then beaten to death with a club.
- **Judas, son of James** (Thaddaeus): Church tradition is not clear on the martyrdom of this apostle. One account states he was crucified, while another tradition claims he was shot to death with arrows.
- **Simon** (the Zealot): The reports of church history tell us that Simon was crucified after preaching the gospel.

If the Resurrection was a lie, a fabrication, don't you think at least one of the apostles would have suddenly exposed such a lie in order to live? Of course they would have. If you were facing death, wouldn't you expose a lie to save your own life? But not one of the apostles changed their story. Why? Because they could not deny what was true. Christ had risen. He was alive!

## THE ABSENCE OF REASONABLE ALTERNATIVE EXPLANATIONS

Because the resurrection of Jesus Christ is essential to the Christian faith, it's easy to see why people have attempted to explain it away. Throughout time, numerous arguments have arisen against the validity of the Resurrection. Let's examine the most common arguments people give as to why the Resurrection did not take place.

### THE SWOON THEORY

*The Premise*

One of the most commonly held theories against the Resurrection is the "swoon theory." This theory proposes that Jesus did not rise from the dead at all, because He actually did not die on the cross. Instead, Jesus went into a deep coma or swooned from the severe pain and trauma of the Crucifixion. Then, in the cool temperature of the tomb, Christ revived, somehow was able to get out of the strips of cloths that were wrapped tightly around Him, and then appeared to His disciples.

*The Rebuttal*

The Roman guards (see "People of the Resurrection") were experts at execution and would be put to death if they allowed a condemned man to escape death. The guards were so certain Jesus was dead, that they did not even bother to break His legs. And when the spear they thrust into Jesus' side brought forth blood and water, they had the final proof of His death, for this occurs when the heart stops beating (see John 19:33-34).

The swoon theory is even less believable when you take into account that Jesus would have had to survive massive blood loss from the scourging, the nail wounds, and the spear thrust from the Roman guard. In addition, Jesus would have had to endure approximately three days without food or drink in His weakened condition. Then in His emaciated state, Jesus would have had to unwrap Himself from His grave clothes (which were glued together hard and fast by the myrrh He was buried with) and then, single-handedly, roll away the massive stone of the tomb. Finally, He would have had to convince His followers that He had risen from the dead—despite His weakened appearance—and travel countless miles in that condition to make many appearances to His disciples over the next forty days.

This theory, understandably, is rarely promoted today. However, there are still some people who conveniently hang their doubt on this theory.

## The No Burial Theory

### *The Premise*

Christ was never put in the tomb to begin with. Instead, He was thrown into a mass grave for criminals, according to Roman custom.

### *The Rebuttal*

If this were true, neither the Jewish leaders nor the Roman soldiers would have bothered to seal the tomb if they knew His body was not located in the tomb (see Matthew 27:62-66). Moreover, to disprove

Jesus' resurrection, they simply had to retrieve the body and display it to the world.

### THE MASS HALLUCINATION THEORY

*The Premise*

Everyone who claimed to see the risen Lord was hallucinating out of an earnest desire to see Jesus alive again.

*The Rebuttal*

Hallucinations typically occur with people who are in one way or another expecting them. But biblical evidence reveals that Jesus' disciples were not expecting to see Him alive again (see Mark 16:10-11). The Resurrection came as a complete and total shock. Additionally, hallucinations, once started, are continual; but the disciples saw Jesus for a limited time and then they ceased to see Him again. Scripture also records that five hundred people saw Christ on a single occasion (see 1 Corinthians 15:6). It is one matter for one person to hallucinate, but a completely different thing for five hundred people to have the identical hallucination simultaneously, which is hardly possible.

## BLESSED ARE THOSE WHO HAVEN'T SEEN ME AND BELIEVE

The Apostle Thomas (see "People of the Resurrection") was skeptical about the Resurrection. He wanted evidence. Eight days after the Resurrection, Christ appeared to Thomas and showed him His nail scars and wounded side. How did Thomas respond? He believed and said, "My Lord and my God!" (John 20:28). Some people might argue that it was easy for Thomas to believe. After all, Thomas saw the risen Lord face to face. But we need to keep in mind Jesus' words to Thomas, "You believe because you have seen me. Blessed are those who haven't seen me and believe anyway" (John 20:29).

The fact of the matter is that belief in Christ is not a case of stacking up the evidence. Many people saw Christ after the Resurrection and still did not believe (for example, see Matthew 28:1-15). Belief in Jesus is founded upon faith. You might say show me and I will believe. For all practical purposes, God says, "Believe and I will show you." Just take a step of faith. All of your questions won't necessarily be answered when you first come to Christ. When I first made my commitment to follow Jesus Christ, I still had questions, problems, and sins that needed to be dealt with. But with as much faith as I had, I took that little step. God more than met me half way. He will do the same for you.

*"Wasn't it clearly predicted by the prophets that the Messiah would have to suffer all these things before entering his time of glory?"*

Luke 24:26

# THE PROPHECIES OF THE RESURRECTION

"PROPHECY IS GOD'S AUTHORITATIVE WORD TO HIS PEOPLE."

Prophecy is God's message to His people and spoken through His chosen prophet. Prophets were women and men of God who experienced a special encounter with the Lord where He directly conveyed His message to them. The prophets experienced these messages through external and internal voices, dreams, and visions, to name a few. Prophecy varied from messages concerning judgment, salvation, assurance, and often times future events.

No matter the content, prophecy is a man or woman of God speaking, proclaiming, or announcing a message under the influence of God's inspiration. Prophecy is God's authoritative word to His people.

## CHRIST PREDICTS HIS RESURRECTION

Jesus Christ (see "People of the Resurrection") repeatedly predicted the Resurrection throughout His ministry. Three days after Christ was crucified, He rose from the dead and fulfilled the Scriptures and the words He spoke concerning the Resurrection.

PROPHESIED: Matthew 12:38-40; 16:4, 21; 17:9, 22-23; 20:17-19; Mark 8:31; 9:9, 31; 10:32-34; Luke 9:22; 11:29-30; 18:31-34; John 2:19-22

FULFILLED: Matthew 27-28; Mark 15-16; Luke 23-24; John 19-20

## CHRIST PREDICTS HIS POST-RESURRECTION MEETING WITH THE DISCIPLES IN GALILEE

The risen Christ met with His disciples in Galilee in order to give hope to His dismayed followers, prove He had risen bodily, and commission them to make disciples of all the nations.

PROPHESIED: Matthew 26:32; Mark 14:28

FULFILLED: Matthew 28:16-20; John 21:1-15

## CHRIST PREDICTS THE ASCENSION

The Ascension signifies Christ's glorification at the right hand of God and the hope for believers that they too will one day ascend into heaven. The Gospel of John records Christ alluding to His ascension, but the disciples and the religious leaders never fully understood the message behind His words.

**PROPHESIED:** John 1:50-51; 7:33-34; 8:14

**FULFILLED:** Mark 16:19; Luke 24:51

## CHRIST PREDICTS THE DAY OF PENTECOST

Pentecost, or Feast of Weeks (see Exodus 34:22 NJKV; Deuteronomy 16:10 NJKV), was a Jewish festival celebrated seven weeks after Passover. In the book of Acts, Pentecost was the day God empowered the first Christians with the Holy Spirit, a day many view as the birth of the church (see Acts 2).

**PROPHESIED:** John 7:37-39; 15:26-27; 16:7; Acts 1:4-5

**FULFILLED:** Acts 2:1-4

## CHRIST PREDICTS THE BIRTH OF THE CHURCH

On Pentecost, the first-century believers were empowered with the Holy Spirit (see Acts 2). This endowed them (and all Christians) with spiritual gifts that enabled them to carry on God's mission and purpose through the collective body of believers known today as the "church."

**PROPHESIED:** Matthew 16:18-19

**FULFILLED:** Acts 2

## OLD TESTAMENT PROPHECIES OF JESUS CHRIST

Included below is a collection of prophecies pertaining to the Resurrection, which was prophesied hundreds, even thousands of years before Christ rose bodily from the dead.

## THE CHRIST WOULD BE RAISED FROM THE DEAD

Long before Jesus was born in the little town of Bethlehem, it was prophesied that the Messiah would rise from the dead.

PROPHESIED: Psalm 16:10

FULFILLED: Matthew 28:2-7

## THE CHRIST WOULD ASCEND TO HEAVEN

Christ's ascension forty days after the Resurrection signified His rightful and exalted place at the right hand of God and provided believers with the hope and confidence needed for Christian living.

PROPHESIED: Psalm 24:7-10

FULFILLED: Mark 16:19; Luke 24:51; Acts 1:9

## THE CHRIST WOULD BE SEATED AT GOD'S RIGHT HAND

Throughout Old Testament times, the right hand of God was the position of honor and exaltation. Christ's place at the right hand of God represents His exalted status in heaven, where He now reigns over creation.

PROPHESIED: Psalm 110:1

FULFILLED: Mark 16:19
See also Matthew 22:44; Hebrews 10:12-13

*"And the disciples went*
*everywhere and preached,*
*and the Lord worked with them,*
*confirming what they said by*
*many miraculous signs."*

Mark 16:20

# THE PEOPLE OF THE RESURRECTION

"THEY ALL MET TOGETHER CONTINUALLY FOR PRAYER, ALONG WITH MARY THE MOTHER OF JESUS, SEVERAL OTHER WOMEN, AND THE BROTHERS OF JESUS." (ACTS 1:14)

## ANDREW

The brother of Simon Peter,* Andrew was a disciple of John the Baptist and was the first of the apostles* to be called by Jesus Christ* (see John 1:35-42). In the events following the Resurrection, Andrew was among the apostles who were present at the Mount of Olives (see "Places of the Resurrection") to witness the ascension of Jesus Christ (see Acts 1:9-13).

## THE APOSTLES

Also known as the "Twelve" and the "disciples," the apostles were men whom Jesus Christ* called and sent out to preach the Good News of the kingdom of God.

1. Peter (Simon)*
2. Andrew (brother of Peter)*

3. James (son of Zebedee)*
4. John (brother of James)*
5. Philip*
6. Bartholomew (Nathanael)*
7. Thomas*
8. Matthew (the tax collector)*
9. James (son of Alphaeus)*
10. Judas, son of James (Thaddaeus)*
11. Simon (the Zealot)*
12. Judas Iscariot (the betrayer)*

Shortly before the Crucifixion, Judas Iscariot* hung himself after the gross realization he had betrayed the Christ, an innocent man who was the Savior of the world (see Matthew 27:3-5). Judas' death is why the apostles are referred to as the Eleven at times (see Matthew 28:16). All four Gospels record Christ, after His resurrection, commissioning and sending out the apostles (see Matthew 28: 18-20; Mark 16:15-16; Luke 24:46-49; John 20:21-23). Though the exact wording of each commission statement varies, the essential message is the same: to be witnesses of Jesus Christ, who carry forth His mission and message (see also Acts 1:22). After Christ ascended into heaven, Matthias* was chosen to replace Judas as the twelfth apostle of Jesus Christ (see Acts 1:16-26).

## BARTHOLOMEW

One of the twelve apostles,* Bartholomew was among the apostles who were present at the Mount of Olives (see "Places of the Resurrection") to witness the ascension of Jesus Christ* (see Acts 1:9-13). Typically, Bartholomew is identified as the disciple Nathanael.*

It is likely that Bartholomew was the disciple Nathanael for the following reasons. First, the Gospels of Matthew, Mark, and Luke all list Bartholomew and Philip together in the naming of the disciples, which suggests they had a close relationship with each other. Secondly, John's Gospel depicts Nathanael as also having a close relationship with Philip, but makes no mention of Bartholomew (see John 1:43-51). A strange omission if Philip was so close to Bartholomew. This leads many to believe that the Nathanael in the fourth Gospel was actually Bartholomew. Lastly, in the Gospel of John, Nathanael is presented as one of the main apostles and all of his friends were apostles as well; however, John makes no mention of the Apostle Bartholomew (see John 1:35-51; 21:1-2). Therefore, a likely conclusion is that Bartholomew and Nathanael were two different names for the same apostle.

## CLEOPAS

Luke 24:18 identifies Cleopas as one of the two disciples who encountered the risen Christ on the road to Emmaus (see "Places of the Resurrection").

## JAMES (SON OF ALPHAEUS)

Sometimes identified as "James the younger" (see Mark 15:40), James was among the apostles* who were present at the Mount of

Olives (see "Places of the Resurrection") to witness the ascension of Jesus Christ* (see Acts 1:9-13).

## JAMES (SON OF ZEBEDEE)

James was the brother of John* and was one of the first apostles* to be called by Jesus Christ.* James, his brother, and Peter* were all part of Jesus' inner circle. He was likely among the disciples who met the risen Christ at the Sea of Galilee (see John 21:1-12). After following Christ to the Mount of Olives (see "Places of the Resurrection"), James was among the privileged group who witnessed Christ ascend in to heaven (see Luke 24:50-52; Acts 1:9-13). James is last mentioned as the first of the apostles to be murdered because of their faith (see Acts 12:2).

## JESUS CHRIST

Jesus of Nazareth was God's promised Christ (anointed one), who was born to die for the sins of the world (see John 3:16). The Gospel of John tells us Jesus existed in the beginning of time and was with God and was God (see John 1:1). Christ was therefore fully God and fully man. He was born of a virgin birth in Bethlehem and raised in Nazareth. He grew up like a normal person, raised by His parents Mary* and Joseph. But unlike the rest of us, Jesus lived a sinless life. He did, however, experience the temptations that everyday people encounter in everyday life (see Matthew 4).

Jesus began His public ministry at the age of thirty. His ministry consisted of the calling of the apostles,* healing the sick, raising the dead, refuting many of the religious leaders, and preaching the kingdom of God and the repentance of sins. He ministered largely in Judea, Samaria, Galilee, and was arrested and condemned in Jerusalem, where He died on the cross for the sins of humankind.

The Crucifixion was not the end of Jesus Christ. Three days later, Christ fulfilled the Scriptures when God raised Him from the dead. This was not a mere resuscitation like Lazarus' rising from the dead. Lazarus would one day die again, but Christ would never face death another time. The Resurrection assures humankind that Christ's death was effective. Sin and death did not defeat Christ, but rather, Christ defeated sin and death. His resurrection means a "new, life-giving way that Christ has opened up for us" (Hebrews 10:20). Believers through Christ are now reconciled to God. The Crucifixion and Resurrection assure believers in Christ that they have the hope of life everlasting.

After the Resurrection, Jesus appeared to His disciples and to five hundred other believers during a period of forty days. During this time, Jesus provided hope to His followers and commissioned them to be His witnesses to the world until He returns again. Forty days after He was raised from the dead, Christ took His disciples to the Mount of Olives where He ascended into heaven. Later, on the day of Pentecost, the Holy Spirit came upon the believers and empowered them to live for God in spirit and in truth.

## JOANNA

Joanna, the wife of Chuza (see Luke 8:3), was a follower of Jesus Christ.* Joanna, who helped provide for Jesus and His disciples while they toured Galilee (see Luke 8:2), was one of the women who prepared spices and ointment for Christ's body. She also discovered the empty tomb along with the other women (see "Places of the Resurrection") and told the story to the disciples, who did not believe what they had to say (see Luke 24:1-11).

## JOHN (THE SON OF ZEBEDEE)

The brother of James* and one of the three members of Jesus' inner circle of disciples, the Apostle John was known as "the disciple whom Jesus Christ loved" (see John 19:26). After hearing about the empty tomb (see "Places of the Resurrection"), John outran Peter* and was the first apostle to see that the tomb was empty (see John 20:3-5). The Apostle Paul later told the church in Galatia that John was one of the three pillars of the church (see Galatians 2:9).

## JOSEPH CALLED BARSABBAS

A follower of Christ, Joseph (called Barsabbas and surnamed Justus) was nominated along with Matthias* to replace Judas Iscariot* (see Acts 1:23). However, the Lord chose Matthias to take Judas' place as the twelfth apostle (see Acts 1:26).

## JUDAS ISCARIOT

Judas Iscariot was the apostle who betrayed Jesus Christ for thirty pieces of silver. He hung himself after realizing the depravity of his actions. The Apostle Peter mentioned Judas when he addressed one hundred and twenty believers in Jerusalem. It was there that Peter and the rest of the apostles* nominated two candidates, Joseph* and Matthias,* to replace Judas. Peter did not speak highly of Judas, saying, "he [Judas] has deserted us and gone where he belongs" (see Acts 1:25).

## JUDAS, SON OF JAMES (THADDAEUS)

The Gospels of Matthew and Mark both name this apostle as Thaddaeus (see Matthew 10:3; Mark 3:18), while the Gospels of Luke and John call him Judas the son of James (see Luke 6:16; Acts 1:13; John 14:22). Judas, more than likely, was his given name while Thaddaeus was a place name or nickname. During the events of the Resurrection, Judas was only mentioned as being present at the Mount of Olives (see "Places of the Resurrection") for Christ's ascension into heaven (see Acts 1:9-13).

## MARY MAGDALENE

A follower of Jesus Christ* from the time He visited cities and villages to announce the Good News of the kingdom of God (see Luke 8:2), Mary was among the last at the cross and the first at Jesus Christ's* tomb on Easter morning. Her status among the women is evident in that she is always listed first when Scripture names groups of the female followers of Christ. All four Gospels record Mary, along with the other female disciples, as the first to discover that Christ's tomb was empty (see Matthew 28:1-10; Mark 16: 1-8; Luke 24:1-12). Mary had the honor of being the first person to whom the resurrected Christ appeared. The Gospel of John records that Jesus commissioned her to find the disciples and proclaim the message: "I have seen the Lord!" (see John 20:14-18).

## MARY, THE MOTHER OF JAMES

Like the other female disciples, Mary was a woman of deep commitment and faith. Comparing the parallel texts of Mark 15:47; 16:1; and Luke 24:10, it is likely that Mary was the "other Mary" of Matthew 27:61 and 28:1. She also was part of the first group of women to appear at the empty tomb (see Matthew 28:1; Mark 16:1; Luke 24:1). With the other female followers, she had the privilege of announcing the news of the Resurrection to the disciples (see Luke 24:10).

## MARY, THE MOTHER OF JESUS

The early portions of the Gospels record that Mary was a young Jewish virgin engaged to a man named Joseph. God had sent the angel Gabriel to announce to her that she was blessed among women (Luke 1:26-38) because He had privileged her with giving birth to the Savior of the world. At the Crucifixion, it was apparent that Jesus Christ's* death would alter the mere mother and son relationship between Jesus and Mary. At the cross, Mary had to accept her new relationship with Christ: the relationship of her as follower and Christ as Lord. After Christ's ascension in to heaven, Mary was present in the upper room (see "Places of the Resurrection"), praying continually with the other disciples (see Acts 1:14).

## MATTHEW (THE TAX COLLECTOR)

Matthew, also called Levi, was a tax collector whom Jesus Christ* called to be His disciple. Matthew responded by leaving everything and following Christ (see Mark 2:14; Luke 5:27-29). Scripture mentions Matthew in all four listings of the apostles* (see Matthew 10:3; Mark 3:18; Luke 6:15; Acts 1:13). He also witnessed Christ's ascension and met for prayer with the other believers in the upper room (see Acts 1:12-14). Matthew also was the author of the Gospel of the same name.

## MATTHIAS

After Christ ascended into heaven, Peter* addressed the need for a twelfth apostle to replace Judas Iscariot.* Peter established a criteria for the election of the twelfth apostle, namely that the candidate would have to have been present from the time John the Baptist baptized Christ to the day Christ ascended into heaven (see Acts 1:21-22). The apostles nominated two men: Matthias and Joseph called Barsabbas.* Using the Old Testament manner for discovering the choice of God (see Proverbs 16:33), the apostles cast lots and chose Matthias (see Acts 1:23-26). No other scriptural information exists concerning Matthias, but church tradition states that he preached in Judea and that he was later stoned to death.

## NATHANAEL

See BARTHOLOMEW.

## PETER (SIMON)

Peter was the famous follower of Jesus Christ* whom the Bible depicts as the leader of the twelve apostles.* Peter's birth name was Simon, but Jesus renamed him *Peter*, which means "rock." Peter and the Apostle John were the first disciples to see the empty tomb (see "Places of the Resurrection") on Easter Sunday (see Luke 24:12; John 20:3-10). Even though during Jesus' trial Peter denied three times that he even knew Jesus, the risen Christ restored Peter and said, "feed my sheep" and "follow me" (see John 21:17, 19).

Peter experienced Christ's ascension into heaven and prayed along with the other disciples in the upper room (see Acts 1:9-14). Shortly thereafter, he addressed the disciples and led them in the nomination and selection of Matthias* as the twelfth apostle. Peter later became one of the central leaders of the early church. He eventually died a martyr's death under Nero's persecution of the Christians.

## PHILIP

Not to be mistaken with Philip the evangelist (see Acts 21:8), Philip was one of the first apostles to follow Christ (see John 1:35-51). Like the other twelve apostles, Philip witnessed the Ascension and was present for the election of Matthias* as the twelfth apostle.

## PONTIUS PILATE

Pontius Pilate was Roman governor (or prefect) of Judea from A.D. 26-36/37 and was a key political figure in the crucifixion of Jesus Christ.*

The day after the Crucifixion, the leading priests and Pharisees came to Pilate and reminded him that Christ had predicted He would rise from the dead in three days. To prevent any birth of resurrection stories, the religious leaders asked Pilate to seal the tomb and have it protected by Roman guards.* This way no one could steal the body of Christ. Pilate appeased the religious leaders and granted their wishes (see Matthew 27:62-66).

But on the third day, an angel rolled away the stone from the tomb, revealing that Christ had indeed risen from the dead (see Matthew 28:1-7). Christ had conquered sin and death! Shortly thereafter, Pilate was recalled from his place of office. Tradition recounts that he later committed suicide.

## THE ROMAN GUARDS

Appointed by Pontius Pilate* to guard Christ's tomb from grave robbers, Scripture says that these men shook with fear when they saw the angel who rolled away the stone from Christ's tomb (see Matthew 28:2-4). The terror of the guards overcame them to the point that "they fell into a dead faint" (Matthew 28:4). As a foil to the positive witness of the women who proclaimed the Resurrection to the disciples, the guards functioned as negative witnesses, telling the leading priests what had happened. The leading priests agreed to bribe the guards, ordering them to lie and say that Jesus' disciples came by night and stole His body (see Matthew 28:11-15).

Unlike the women's reverent fear of God, which was followed by great joy (see Matthew 28:8), the guards experienced a fear of God that all enemies of the Lord will ultimately face.

## SALOME

A faithful follower of Jesus Christ,* Salome helped care for Christ while in Galilee. Along with Mary Magdalene* and Mary the mother of James,* Salome brought spices to anoint Christ's body for burial and discovered that He had risen from the dead (see Mark 16:1-8).

## SIMON (THE ZEALOT)

One of the twelve apostles* of Jesus Christ,* Simon was a member of the Zealots, a revolutionary political group that believed political submission to Rome denied God as Lord. The Gospels of Matthew and Mark in the Greek refer to Simon as the "Cananaean," which is from the Aramaic word for *Zealot* (see Matthew 10:4; Mark 3:18). The dynamics of the apostles are apparent with the call of Simon the Zealot and Matthew the tax collector.* Tax collectors and Zealots were on opposite ends of the political spectrum. After the Resurrection, Simon, like the rest of the eleven apostles, was present for Christ's ascension into heaven, the corporate prayer in the upper room, and the election of Matthias as Judas' replacement (see Acts 1:12-26).

## THADDAEUS

See JUDAS (SON OF JAMES).

## THOMAS

Improperly known as "doubting Thomas," the Gospel of John depicts this apostle as a strong, faithful, and courageous man of character. Thomas' boldness is evident in his words to the apostles,* "Let's go, too–and die with Jesus" (John 11:16). But he is most famous for missing the first appearance of the risen Christ (see John 20:19-24), and then refusing to believe that Jesus was alive until he saw Jesus Christ* and the wounds on His body. Eight days later, Jesus granted Thomas' request and appeared before him and the other disciples. Jesus said to Thomas, "Put your finger here and see my hands. Put your hand into the wound in my side. Don't be faithless any longer. Believe!" (John 20: 27). Thomas replied with one of the New Testament's most profound and monumental confessions of Christ's deity: "My Lord and my God!" (John 20: 28). Afterward, Thomas was present with the other apostles for the Ascension, the corporate prayer in the upper room, and the election of Matthias as the replacement of Judas Iscariot* as the twelfth apostle (see Acts 1:1-26).

*"Suddenly there was a great earthquake, because an angel of the Lord came down from heaven and rolled aside the stone . . . ."*

Matthew 28:2

# THE PLACES OF THE RESURRECTION

"VERY EARLY ON SUNDAY MORNING THE WOMEN CAME TO THE TOMB, TAKING THE SPICES THEY HAD PREPARED. THEY FOUND THAT THE STONE COVERING THE ENTRANCE HAD BEEN ROLLED ASIDE." (LUKE 24:1-2)

## BETHANY

Bethany, a city located off of the Jericho road less than two miles from Jerusalem,* was positioned on the southeast slopes of the Mount of Olives.* In his Gospel, Luke writes that the ascension of Jesus Christ (see "People of the Resurrection") transpired in Bethany: "Then Jesus led them to Bethany, and lifting his hands to heaven, he blessed them. While he was blessing them, he left them and was taken up to heaven" (24:50-51). In Acts, Luke places the Ascension at the Mount of Olives (see Acts 1:9-12). This difference in detail poses no significant problems since Bethany sat at the foot of the Mount of Olives.*

## THE EMPTY TOMB

The Garden Tomb was the burial site of Jesus Christ. Unlike tombs today, this tomb was carved out of a rock with the entrance covered by a large stone. Luke, in his Gospel, tells us that it was a new tomb where no one had ever been laid (see Luke 23:53). All four Gospels record the female followers of Christ appearing at the tomb early Sunday morning, only to find it empty. It was there that the angel proclaimed the message of the Resurrection, and hope was restored to all of Christ's followers (see Matthew 28:1-10; Mark 16:1-8; Luke 24:1-12; John 20:1-17).

## EMMAUS

A village seven miles out of Jerusalem,* Emmaus was the destination of two discouraged disciples, Cleopas (see "People of the Resurrection") and another unnamed disciple (see Luke 24:13-18). There on the Emmaus road, the two disciples encountered a stranger who asked them about their conversation concerning Jesus of Nazareth. The stranger was none other than the risen Lord. The two disciples were unable to recognize Jesus, because God had kept them from realizing who He was.

While walking on the road, Jesus taught them everything that the writings of Moses and the prophets said concerning the Christ. Later that day, Cleopas and the other follower begged Christ to stay the night with them because it was getting late (see Luke 24:29). When the three of them sat down to eat, Christ blessed the food and suddenly "their eyes were opened, and they recognized him" (see Luke 24:30-31). At that moment of discovery, Jesus disappeared!

Within the hour, the two witnesses of the risen Christ were traveling back to Jerusalem. Upon their arrival, they heard other accounts of the resurrected Lord and then reported to the Eleven their meeting with the risen Lord. Just then, Jesus appeared before the group, showed them His nail-pierced hands and feet so they would know He was no ghost (see Luke 24:33-40). He had truly risen bodily from the dead.

## FIELD OF BLOOD (*AKELDAMA*)

Also known as "Potter's Field," the leading priests purchased this plot of land with the thirty pieces of silver that Judas Iscariot (see "People of the Resurrection") returned to them. The priests were not able to return the money to the Temple* treasury because it had been used to pay for murder (see Matthew 27:1-10). Instead, they bought with it the Potter's Field and used it as a cemetery for foreigners.

In Acts, Peter referred to the "Field of Blood" when he announced the need to elect a new apostle to replace Judas Iscariot (see Acts 1:16-21). Luke provides his readers with the knowledge that it was Judas' betrayal of Christ that ultimately funded the purchase of the "Field of Blood" (see Acts 1:18-19).

## THE FIRST CENTURY TEMPLE (19 B.C.–A.D. 64)

The Jerusalem Temple was the center of religious and social life for the Jews of Christ's day. Herod the Great built the Temple in order to appease the Jews and rival Solomon's Temple, which King Nebuchadnezzar burned in 587 B.C. The Temple was an ornate, cream-colored

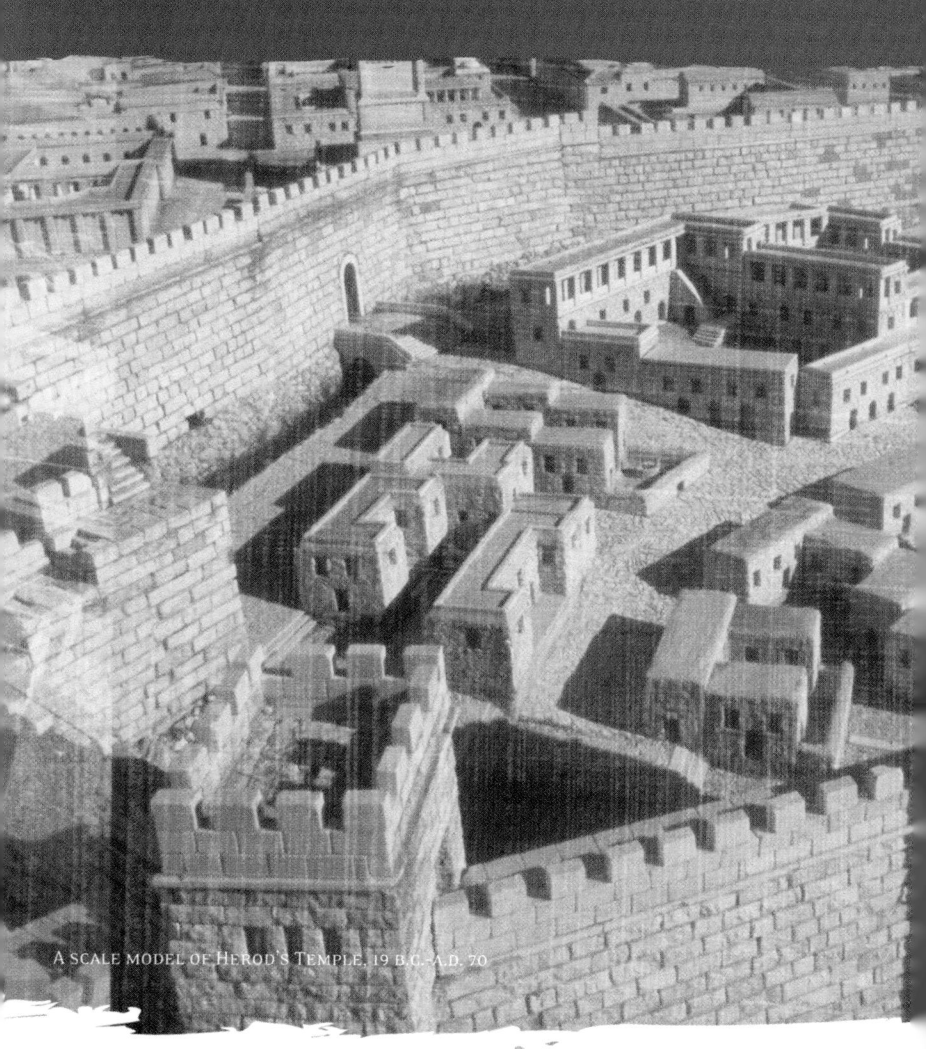
A SCALE MODEL OF HEROD'S TEMPLE, 19 B.C.–A.D. 70

house of worship that filled an area measuring approximately 490 yards from north to south and 325 yards from east to west. The main construction of the Temple was finished in 9 B.C. with the final construction ending in A.D. 64. Seven years later, the Romans utterly annihilated the Herodian Temple.

"I will
**DESTROY**
this **TEMPLE**
made with
human hands,
and in
**THREE DAYS**
I will build another,
made without
human **HANDS**"

MARK 14:58

In his Gospel, Luke writes that after Jesus ascended into heaven, the disciples went to Jerusalem and "spent all of their time in the Temple, praising God" (Luke 24:53). Once the Holy Spirit came upon the believers, the book of Acts says that they "worshiped together at the Temple each day . . . all the while praising God . . . ." (2:46, 47).

## GALILEE

The location of Jesus Christ's childhood (Nazareth, which is in lower Galilee), Galilee was the primary setting of Jesus' ministry. He taught ten of His thirty-two parables and performed twenty-five of His thirty-three miracles there. Jesus soon recognized that the major centers of Galilee were not receptive to the gospel, so He denounced such Galilean cities as Korazin, Bethsaida, and Capernaum (see Matthew 11:21-24). He and His disciples then began proclaiming the kingdom of God in regions outside of Galilee (see Mark 7:24, 31; 8:27).

After rising from the dead, Jesus told the female disciples to tell the other disciples to go to Galilee—for they would see Him there (see Matthew 28:10). Two of the most monumental appearances of Christ occurred in Galilee. First, Jesus appeared to several of His disciples at the Sea of Galilee. It was then that He restored Peter (see "People of the Resurrection") and said, "Follow me" (see John 21:15-19). Also in Galilee, Christ commissioned the apostles (see "People of the Resurrection") to "make disciples of all the nations, baptizing them in the name of the Father and the Son and the Holy Spirit" (see Matthew 28:16-20).

## JERUSALEM

The famous capital of Palestine during Old Testament times, Jerusalem had been conquered by the Romans and was reduced to a city-state by the time of the New Testament.

Jerusalem was the location of Jesus Christ's arrest, conviction, and crucifixion. After the Resurrection, Jerusalem became the setting of the following important events:

- Jesus' appearance to the two disciples on the Emmaus road (see Mark 16:12)
- Jesus' appearance to the Eleven (see John 20:19-25)
- the ascension of Christ (see Luke 24:50-52; Acts 1:9-12)
- the prayer meeting in the upper room (see Acts 1:13-14)
- Pentecost (see Acts 2:1-4)

## THE MOUNT OF OLIVES

The Mount of Olives is a rounded hill reaching 2,676 feet high and overlooked the Temple.* In Christ's final week, He taught on the Mount of Olives and spent His nights there (see Mark 13; Luke 21:37). His final earthly event also occurred on the Mount of Olives. It was there that He ascended into heaven, as His disciples watched in amazement (see Acts 1:12).

## THE SEA OF GALILEE

Famous for being the setting of many New Testament events (see Matthew 8:23-27; Mark 5:1-13, 35-41; Luke 8:22-25; John 6:16-21), the Sea of Galilee is located in the Jordan Valley, its surface sits at 696 feet below sea level. This body of water is approximately thirteen miles long and eight miles wide.

After Jesus rose from the dead, He appeared to the disciples as they were fishing at the Sea of Galilee. Jesus yelled out to them, asking, "Friends, have you caught any fish?" (John 21:5). Unable to see who He was, the disciples told Him no and were directed by Christ to cast their net on the right side of the boat. The disciples obeyed and caught so many fish that they were not able to draw in the net (see John 21:6). Suddenly, they realized that the man standing on the shore was Jesus, their Lord (see John 21:7-13).

## THE UPPER ROOM

In biblical times, some homes had second-story rooms, which resembled towers. These rooms were often referred to as "upper rooms." After the Ascension, Luke wrote that the apostles returned to Jerusalem and went to the upper room of the house where they were staying (see Acts 1:12-13). It was most likely there that the apostles prayed continually with the other followers of Christ (see Acts 1:14).

## THE APPEARANCES OF THE RISEN CHRIST

To help unfold the events between Christ's resurrection and ascension, below is a chronology of the ten appearances of the risen Christ as recorded in Scripture.

| SUMMARY OF EVENTS | THE PLACE |
|---|---|
| Christ appears to Mary Magdalene and commissions her to tell the disciples about His soon-coming ascension. | The Garden Tomb |
| On their way to tell the disciples about the Resurrection, Jesus appears to the women and commands them to tell the disciples to go to Galilee. | A Road near Jerusalem |
| Cleopas and another disciple encounter Christ without recognizing Him. When they realize it is Jesus, they go and tell the others. | The Road to Emmaus |
| Cleopas and the other disciple arrive in Jerusalem and are greeted with the news that Christ appeared to the Apostle Peter. | Unknown |
| Christ appears to Cleopas and the other disciples, eats with them, teaches them the Scriptures, and tells them to preach to all the nations. | Behind Locked Doors |
| Christ shows Himself to Thomas and the other disciples, providing Thomas the opportunity to see His wounds and believe in Him. | Behind Locked Doors |
| Peter, Thomas, Nathanael, John, James, and two other disciples see Jesus while fishing. There Christ challenges Peter and says, "Follow me." | The Sea of Galilee |
| Christ meets the eleven disciples, and perhaps hundreds of others (see 1 Corinthians 15:6-7), and gives them the Great Commission. | An Unnamed Mountain |
| Christ appears to the eleven disciples as they are eating, rebukes them, and commands them to preach the Good News to everyone. | Unknown |
| Christ leads the eleven disciples to Bethany on the Mount of Olives, promises them the Holy Spirit, and ascends into heaven. | The Mount of Olives |

| THE TIME | THE SCRIPTURE |
|---|---|
| Early Easter Morning, While It Was Still Dark | John 20:11-18 |
| Early Easter Morning | Matthew 28:5-10. See also Mark 16:2-8; Luke 24:1-11 |
| Easter around Noon | Mark 16:12-13; Luke 24:13-35 |
| Easter Day | Luke 24:34; 1 Corinthians 15:5 |
| Easter Evening | Luke 24:35-49; John 20:19-23 |
| Eight Days after Easter | John 20:24-29 |
| At Dawn, between Easter and the Ascension | John 21:1-25 |
| Between Easter and the Ascension | Matthew 28:16-20 |
| Between Easter and the Ascension | Mark 16:14-18 |
| Forty Days after Easter | Luke 24:50-53; Acts 1:4-11 |

*"Therefore, go and make disciples of all the nations, baptizing them in the name of the Father and the Son and the Holy Spirit."*

Matthew 28:19

# THE GREAT COMMISSION

"THE KNOWLEDGE OF CHRIST'S COMMISSION SETS A CHOICE BEFORE US. WE CAN EVANGELIZE OR WE CAN FOSSILIZE."

## CONVERSION IS THE WORK OF GOD

I once heard a story about a time when Billy Graham was traveling by plane. There was a very inebriated man on the flight who heard the famed evangelist was on board. Eager to meet Dr. Graham, the gentleman got up out of his seat and with a slurred voice announced, "I want to meet Billy Graham!" One of the flight attendants attempted to control the situation by telling him, "Sir, you have to take your seat." But the man still insisted, "I want to meet Billy Graham!" As his voice grew louder, Billy overheard the commotion, got up out of his seat, and stepped into the aisle to greet the gentleman. The man fiercely shook his hand and boasted, "Billy Graham, you don't know how much your preaching has helped me." Billy thought to himself, *It couldn't have helped him too much.*

There are countless people today who will profess faith in Christ, but do not reflect it in their lifestyle. Conversion is the work of God, but throughout Scripture He has used human instruments to bring about the salvation of the lost. The fact of the matter is that God uses willing Christians to perform His will.

I recently read an alarming statistic that 95 percent of all Christians have never led another person to Jesus Christ (see "People of the Resurrection"). It is interesting to wonder if this is because Christians are out there trying and haven't had the blessing of seeing someone come to Christ? Or is it because few of us are trying and many of us have never even spoken up? Sadly, I think it is the latter of the two. Granted, God is the only One who can bring about the conversion of a person. I can't do it. You can't do it. Only God can. But somehow He involves us in the process.

This is why we need to ask ourselves whether or not we have done our part. Have we made ourselves available to the work of evangelism? Have we planted that seed or at least made an attempt?

## THE GREAT COMMISSION

I know that for some the idea of evangelism can seem daunting and overwhelming. But as we come to the Scriptures, we will see that God has provided us with the authority and power to reach this lost world—one person at a time. Before Christ ascended into heaven, He told His disciples how. Let's read about it in Matthew 28:18-20:

> Jesus came and told his disciples, "I have been given complete authority in heaven and on earth. Therefore, go and make dis-

> ciples of all the nations, baptizing them in the name of the Father and the Son and the Holy Spirit. Teach these new disciples to obey all the commands I have given you. And be sure of this: I am with you always, even to the end of the age."

There are two very important things to consider in this statement of our Lord. First, in the original language it is a command. That is why we refer to this statement of the Lord as the Great Commission and not the "great suggestion." It was not a suggestion of Jesus that we carry the gospel into all nations. It was and is a command.

Secondly, these words were not merely directed to the original Eleven. They were given to all followers of the Lord. Sometimes we may think that evangelism should be left to the so called professionals—the pastors, the evangelists, preachers, and missionaries. You may think, "I am not really called to be an evangelist." That may be true, but every believer is called to evangelize.

Unfortunately, instead of fulfilling the Great Commission, some of us are guilty of the "great omission." As followers of Christ, we need to recognize that Scripture teaches that there are sins of commission and omission. A sin of commission involves doing what you should not do. A sin of omission is not doing what you should do. We might pride ourselves on the fact that we have not broken certain commandments or have not done certain things that Scripture forbids. But we are failing to realize that not sharing the gospel can also be a sin. It is a sin of omission. The Bible says, "Remember, it is sin to know what you ought to do and then not do it" (James 4:17). Our Lord has commanded us to go and share the gospel message with the lost. But how, how do we obtain the power and courage to share God's love with this world? The answer is through Christ.

## BE A DISCIPLE MAKER

Jesus said, "*Therefore*, go and make disciples of all the nations" (Matthew 28:19, emphasis mine). Whenever you see the word *therefore*, find out what it is there for. It is drawing upon what has previously been said. What did Jesus say prior to this? He said to the other disciples, "I have been given complete authority in heaven and on earth" (Matthew 28:18). Jesus was making a connection. The connection is that all the power in all of the world and the universe is in Christ. He is over all things. Now consider this: His Spirit lives in you. In other words, He will give you the power to achieve what He has called you to do. God's calling is also His enabling. Sharing God's love is not for you to live out in your own strength. He is going to accomplish it through you as you yield to the Holy Spirit. Therefore, go and preach the gospel. For the sake of those who don't know Christ, go *therefore* and make disciples.

What does it mean to make disciples? Jesus defined it in verse 20, "Teach these new disciples to obey all the commands I have given you." To make disciples of all the nations means to teach people to observe what Jesus commanded. It is to live our faith in this world and share it with others, teaching it by word and modeling it by example. This concept of making disciples is the willing action of trying to win people to the Lord and then get them up on their feet spiritually. The Apostle Paul substantiated this when he wrote, "So everywhere we go, we tell everyone about Christ. We warn them and teach them with all the wisdom God has given us, for we want to present them to God, perfect in their relationship to Christ" (Colossians 1:28). This is what we need to do–help people come to faith and help them grow in their faith spiritually. This is the Great Commission.

But the knowledge of Christ's commission presents us with a choice. We can evangelize or we can fossilize. If you are only taking in the truth of God and don't have an outlet for your newfound truth, you can begin to spiritually stagnate. If you know someone who is young in the faith and is discovering these things for the first time, it can reinvigorate and even bring personal, spiritual revival to your own life.

You may think you do not know enough to share your faith with another person. I suggest you know a lot more than you may realize. The average Christian has a lot of embedded truth that has never been utilized. And if you don't feel as though you know what you need to know, equip yourself. For the Bible says "Set apart Christ as Lord. Always be prepared to give an answer to everyone who asks you to give the reason for the hope that you have. But do this with gentleness and respect" (1 Peter 3:15 NIV).

I also would encourage you to get a copy of the *New Believer's Bible.* I had the privilege of writing the notes for this Bible, and as you carefully study what is there, you will better equip yourself to the task of effectively sharing the gospel message.

## THE HARVEST IS GREAT

Today, ask yourself, *When was the last time I initiated a conversation about my faith?* We all need to put up our little spiritual antennas and pray, "Lord, I'm available. Call on me today. Use me." Those opportunities are out there. You only have to be willing, and the Lord will use you to make disciples.

Before Jesus died and rose again, He told His disciples, "The harvest is so great, but the workers are so few. So pray to the Lord who is in charge of the harvest; ask him to send out more workers for his fields" (Matthew 9:37-38). We, as believers, are God's workers. God has chosen to work through human instruments. He has chosen to use people just like you and just like me. You are someone God wants to work through, and indeed can use, to bring the life-changing message of the gospel to this generation. Will you be open? Will you be available? The opportunities are there. But it is up to us to seize them.

*"You are a chosen*

*people. You are*

*a kingdom of priests,*

*God's holy nation,*

*his very*

*own possession."*

1 Peter 2:9

# THE BIRTH OF THE CHURCH

"JESUS WANTS TODAY'S CHURCH TO HAVE A PROFOUND IMPACT ON ITS CULTURE, TO TURN THE WORLD UPSIDE DOWN FOR CHRIST."

## THE TRUE SOURCE OF OUR STRENGTH

One night, several years ago, hurricane-enforced winds battered an American town. In the morning, people emerged from their homes and shelters to assess the damage. The power of the storm quickly became apparent to one investigator, who was baffled by an amazing discovery. Imbedded in a telephone pole, he found a flimsy, plastic drinking straw. Obviously, under normal circumstances, a straw could never penetrate a telephone pole. The tremendous power of the wind is what drove that straw like a spike into the wood.

Christians are similar to that drinking straw. Apart from the power of the Holy Spirit, we could never impact our world for Christ. It is the power of the Holy Spirit that enables us to love our neighbor, forgive one another, and preach the Good News. This is why Jesus Christ (see "People of the Resurrection") left the disciples. He left so He could send the Holy Spirit to empower all believers.

During the forty days between the Resurrection and the Ascension, Christ appeared to His disciples a number of times. He was there for His followers to reach out and touch. Can you imagine being one of those believers who walked and talked with the Lord? Those first-century believers could hear Christ's voice with their own ears and see Him with their own eyes.

But the disciples were still confused about Christ's purpose for the world even with the risen Lord before their very eyes. They thought He was going to free Israel from Roman rule and restore their kingdom (see Acts 1:6). But what occurred forty days after the Resurrection amazed Christ's disciples. Instead of overturning the Roman government, Jesus led the disciples up to the Mount of Olives (see "Places of the Resurrection"), blessed them, and ascended into heaven. Two angels then appeared afterward and signaled to them that this was the last time Christ would appear to them in this fashion. The angels asked the disciples, "Men of Galilee, why are you standing here staring at the sky? Jesus has been taken away from you into heaven. And someday, just as you saw him go, he will return!" (Acts 1:11). The angels revealed to the disciples that their Lord was now in heaven sitting in His exalted place at the right hand of God. There He would rule until He returned again at the Second Coming. Jesus' purpose was spiritual, while the disciples' purpose was political.

## YOU WILL RECEIVE POWER

Jesus, however, did not leave His disciples without direction. Just before He ascended into heaven, He reminded them of the promise concerning the Holy Spirit. There on the Mount of Olives, He proclaimed, "But when the Holy Spirit has come upon you, you will receive power and will tell people about me everywhere—in Jerusalem, throughout Judea, in Samaria, and to the ends of the earth" (Acts 1:8). That promise was fulfilled on the day of Pentecost. Seven weeks after the Resurrection, the Holy Spirit came upon the disciples and transformed their lives. The coming of the Holy Spirit impacted their lives to the point that they could not keep it to themselves. As Peter and John (see "People of the Resurrection") said, "We cannot stop telling about the wonderful things we have seen and heard" (Acts 4:20).

This power that the first-century Christians experienced is also available to believers today. The Holy Spirit comes to live in every person who has put their faith in Christ. The Holy Spirit seals us. He dwells in us. But there is a dimension of this power promised that will better enable us, as Christ's followers, to be witnesses for Him. Every Christian needs this power to be the person God has called them to be. It's a supernatural courage to stand up and be counted. And God can give us this boldness today.

The early church was completely dependent upon the work of the Holy Spirit. They were dependent upon God using them. They didn't have many of the advantages that we have today, if you even want to call them that. They didn't have technology like printing presses, radio, television, and the Internet. But the early church possessed the power of God's Spirit in their lives.

Occasionally when we think of the power of the Spirit we get a little concerned. We all have seen abuses in this area by some people who engage in unusual and sometimes flat-out bizarre behavior that they attribute to the Holy Spirit. But I want you to know that God doesn't provide His power for us merely to have an emotional experience. He doesn't give us that power just so we can feel good about ourselves or simply have a wonderful time at church. It's a practical power to go out and impact this world that we are living in.

I think we need to ask for this power in our lives. I think every one of us should pray for God to fill us with His Spirit today. For some of us it will be the first time we have ever received this dimension of power to be a witness for Jesus Christ. For others, we need a refill. Did you know God likes to give refills? For instance, when you run out of gas, you don't say, "Time to get rid of the car. It ran out of gas." No, when the car is out of gas, that simply means it's time to get a refill. In the same way, the Bible tells us in Ephesians 5:18, "Let the Holy Spirit fill and control you." In the original language that could be better translated "Be constantly filled with the Holy Spirit." The Holy Spirit is Someone we need in our lives.

Through the Holy Spirit, the early believers—the church—began to turn their world upside down. They challenged the rulers of their land, preached in uncharted territory, and many even died for their faith—all empowered by God's Spirit. Indeed, that is what Jesus wants the church—the collective body of Christian believers—to do. Like that small group of first-century Christians, Jesus wants today's church to have a profound impact on its culture, to turn the world upside down for Him (see Acts 17:6). It is possible—if we do it in God's way and in God's power.

## GOD'S PURPOSE FOR THE CHURCH

As believers empowered by the Holy Spirit and members of the body of Christ, God has a purpose for us. We need to be aware of God's will and desire for His church. In other words, is the church's primary purpose to help meet the needs of you and your family? Is it here to win the world for Christ? Does it exist to right the world of social wrongs? Or is it a hospital for saints and sinners? You might be surprised by the Bible's answer. None of these suggestions alone is the reason the church exists.

*I believe the church is on this earth for three reasons:*

1. Exalt God
2. Edify believers
3. Evangelize the lost

*Another way to put it is:*

1. Upward (Exaltation)
2. Inward (Edification)
3. Outward (Evangelization)

The first purpose of the church is to exalt God. This is the Christian's upward focus in life. God put us on this earth to know Him and to glorify Him (see Ephesians 1:12). That idea may come as a revelation to some people. Many people think they are on this earth to make their mark on society, or they may think their purpose is to go out and merely find a career and become successful. Others feel their reason for living is to have a family or find personal happiness. But the Bible teaches that we are put on this earth primarily to know and bring glory to the God who created us. Peter pointed this purpose out when he wrote, "You are a chosen people. You are a kingdom of priests, God's holy nation, his very own possession. This is so you can show others the goodness of God, for he called you out of the darkness into his wonderful light" (1 Peter 2:9). As you can see, the Bible is clear that the church exists to exalt and praise God. First and foremost, our relationships in life should be focused upward.

The second function of the church is to concentrate inward. This means the church is to edify other believers in the body of Christ. The Apostle Paul said that his goal was not merely to evangelize, but to "warn them [believers] and teach them with all the wisdom God has given us, for we want to present them to God, perfect in their relationship to Christ" (Colossians 1:28). That is why we are here. That is what church is about. The church doesn't exist just to sing a few songs, teach a message, and give an offering. We are here to be equipped and equip one another. Only as mature, Spirit-filled believers, can we have the maximum impact on the world for God's glory.

Lastly, God has called the church to go outward. In other words, we are to go into all the world and evangelize the lost. This purpose is a natural outgrowth of the first two. If we are exalting God and edifying one another, we will naturally want to share the hope of salvation with others through our loving actions and words. We also will want to obey the Lord. Healthy sheep will reproduce themselves. This was Christ's commandment before He ascended into heaven: "Go into all the world and preach the Good News to everyone, everywhere" (Mark 16:15). The church should do just that.

It is essential that we keep these principles in their proper balance. The church is not to emphasize one principle at the expense of the other or take them out of their proper order. The church has to have balance. It needs to exalt God, it needs to edify the believers, and it needs to evangelize the lost. All of these principles must be emphasized on a regular basis to keep the church strong and healthy.

## TURNING THE WORLD UPSIDE DOWN

Maintaining the proper balance of the church would be impossible on our own strength. But on the Day of Pentecost, God provided believers in Christ with the strength to do so through the Holy Spirit. We can't do it on our own, but by being energized and empowered by God's Spirit we can do all things through the strength of Jesus Christ (see Philippians 4:13). That's why we need to say, "Lord, there is no way we can impact our culture in our own strength. We can't do it through programs. We can't do it through gimmicks. We can't do it through any of our own devices. We need a power beyond ourselves. We need to be like that little straw thrust into a telephone pole by the power of a hurricane. Lord, we are flimsy. We are weak. We can't do it on our own. But with Your power launching us into this culture, we can make a difference. We need You in our lives."

It is my prayer that we—the church—will pray for the Holy Spirit to bring power into our lives so that we might turn our world upside down for the Lord.

*"But the fact is that*

*Christ has been raised*

*from the dead.*

*He has become the first*

*of a great harvest of*

*those who will*

*be raised to life again."*

1 Corinthians 15:20

# LIFE AFTER DEATH

"IT WAS SO WONDERFUL FOR ME TO REALIZE THAT THERE WAS A GOD WHO LOVED ME, AND THERE ALSO WAS PROMISE OF ETERNAL LIFE."

Before I became a Christian, it was my belief that when a person died, he or she simply ceased to exist. I had no hope at all of an eternal future, and, quite honestly, it was a terrifying concept. I thought, "How could I simply cease to exist?" When I came to faith in Christ, it was so wonderful for me to realize that there was a God who loved me, and there also was promise of eternal life.

Just as Christ's death and resurrection changed everything for me, you too can experience the life-changing message of the gospel. If you too want the assurance that when you die, you will experience life after death, then there are a few things I would like to share with you.

## FIRST, REALIZE THAT YOU ARE A SINNER

No matter how good a life we try to live, we still will fall miserably short of God's standards.

The Bible says, "No one is good—not even one" (Romans 3:10). Another word for *good* is *righteous*. The word *righteous* means "one who is as he or she ought to be." Apart from Jesus Christ, we cannot become the people we "ought to be."

## SECOND, RECOGNIZE THAT JESUS CHRIST DIED ON THE CROSS FOR YOU

Scripture says, "But God showed his great love for us by sending Christ to die for us while we were still sinners" (Romans 5:8). God gave His very Son to die in our place when we least deserved it. As the Apostle Paul said, "[Christ] loved me and gave himself for me" (Galatians 2:20).

## THIRD, REPENT OF YOUR SIN

The Bible tells us to "repent . . . and be converted" (Acts 3:19). The word *repent* means to change our direction in life. Instead of running from God, we can run toward Him.

## FOURTH, RECEIVE JESUS CHRIST INTO YOUR LIFE

Becoming a Christian is not merely believing some creed or going to church on Sunday. It is having Christ Himself take residence in your life and heart. Jesus said, "Behold, I stand at the door [of your life] and knock. If anyone hears My voice and opens the door, I will come in . . ." (Revelation 3:20 NKJV).

Jesus stands at the door of your life right now and is knocking. He says that if you will hear His voice and open the door, He will come in. If you would like to know that when you die you will go to heaven, and if you want to have a life that is full of purpose and meaning, then pray this suggested prayer and mean it with your heart:

*Dear Lord Jesus, I know I am a sinner.*

*I believe You died for my sins and rose again*

*from the dead. Right now, I turn from my sins*

*and open the door of my heart and life.*

*I confess You as my personal Lord and Savior.*

*Thank you for saving me.*

*Amen.*

A LETTER FROM GREG LAURIE

EAR FRIEND,

If you just prayed that prayer and meant it, then Jesus Christ has now taken residence in your heart! Your decision to follow Christ means God has forgiven you and that you will spend eternity in heaven. The Bible tells us, “If we confess our sins, He is faithful and just to forgive us our sins and to cleanse us from all unrighteousness” (1 John 1:9 NKJV).

To put your faith in action, be sure to spend time with God by reading the Bible, praying, going to church, and telling others about Christ. To help you with your faith, you can receive spiritual resources from Harvest Ministries by writing us or by registering your decision at our Web site at www.harvest.org/knowgod. While you’re at our Web site, be sure to visit the “Tools for Spiritual Growth” page. There you’ll discover biblical teachings and resources that will encourage you as you learn to know God and share His love with others.

May God bless you as you grow closer to Him.

Sharing God’s love,

Greg Laurie

PS: You can e-mail me personally at Greg@harvest.org.

HARVEST MINISTRIES P.O. BOX 4000
RIVERSIDE, CA 92514

WWW.HARVEST.ORG

# ABOUT THE AUTHOR

GREG LAURIE IS THE SENIOR PASTOR of Harvest Christian Fellowship in Riverside, California, one of the ten largest churches in America. A gifted evangelist and Bible teacher, Greg has a passionate desire to see people come to Christ and become established in their Christian faith. He conducts evangelistic outreaches known as Harvest Crusades and is the featured speaker on the nationally syndicated radio and television program *A New Beginning*. Greg has written a number of books including *Why Believe? How to Share Your Faith,* and *New Believer's Guide to the Bible.* The *New Believer's One Year Bible,* containing helpful notes for those new to the Bible, will be released in 2005.

COMPANION BOOK

# *Why the Passion?*

Just days ago He had been hailed as King. Worshippers laid their clothes on the road before Him. But Jesus was on His way to Jerusalem. He knew the events of His mission on earth would unfold shortly.

Why did Jesus Christ suffer the Passion? The crucifixion of Jesus Christ is undoubtedly one of the most important events in human history. *Why the Passion?* presents you with a firsthand look at the people, the places, and the politics behind this event and how it has had eternal ramifications for all of humanity.

In *Why the Passion?* Greg Laurie takes you through the experience of the Passion and what it means for people past, present, and in the future. He provides you with biblically accurate information on . . .

- Why Jesus Christ had to die
- The prophecies concerning the death of Jesus Christ
- A chronology of the main events of the last twelve hours of Jesus Christ's life

You've discovered the power of the Risen Lord. Now go back and read *Why the Passion?* to experience Jesus Christ's Passion to save us from our sins.